"Bocage" and Other Sonnets

"Bocage" and Other Sonnets

William Baer

Texas Review Press
Huntsville, Texas

FIRST EDITION, 2008
Requests for permission to reproduce material from this work should
be sent to:

Permissions
Texas Review Press
English Department
Sam Houston State University
Huntsville, TX 77341-2146

ACKNOWLEDGMENTS:

Best of the Midwest: "Intruder"
Bryant Literary Review: "The Shower"
Connecticut Review: "Dream," "Nightmare," and "The Naughty
    Sonnet"
Crisis: "Pharaoh"
The Hudson Review: "Chocolate"
First Things: "The Widow of Niam"
The Kenyon Review: "Arrhythmia"
Knockout: "Like a Speeding Bullet"
The London Magazine (England): "Fog" and "Bookstore"
Michigan Quarterly Review: "Illiterate Love Note" and Martinique"
Modern Age: "Continuum"
National Review: "Bocage," "Eve," "Lover," "Archaeologist," and
    "Reception"
New York Quarterly: "Seaside Heights"
Ploughshares: "Motes" and "The Puzzle House"
Stand (England): "The Spot," "Clerical Error," and "Impersonator"
The Raintown Review: "Dictionary" and "Blood Splatter"
The South Carolina Review: "Letter of Resignation"
Southwest Review: "Cartographer"
Quadrant (Australia): "Elevator" and "International Dateline"
The Wanderer: "Judah," "Theotokos," and "Herod"

Cover graphic by David Markowitz (dave@artfoundry.com)
Cover design by Paul Ruffin

Library of Congress Cataloging-in-Publication Data

Baer, William, 1948-
  Bocage and other sonnets / William Baer.
    p. cm.
  ISBN-13: 978-1-933896-19-9 (pbk. : alk. paper)
  ISBN-10: 1-933896-19-1
  I. Title.
  PS3552.A3324B63 2008
  811'.54–dc22
                              2008031024

For my family and friends
(especially Margaret Baer)

CONTENTS

I.

Bocage—1
The "2" Train—2
Cartographer—3
Chocolate—4
Motes—5
Arrhythmia—6
The Puzzle House—7
Zermatt—8
The Naughty Sonnet—9

II. From Cecília Meireles

The Rain Rains—13
Herod—14
Spider Hole—15
Joan of Arc—16
Coimbra Night—17

III.

Seaside Heights—21
Blood Splatter—22
Post Card—23
Reception—24
Intruder—25
Martinique—26
Elevator—27
Fog—28
Illiterate Love Note—29
Impersonator—30
Letter of Resignation—31

IV. Sermons (to Myself)

Eve—35

Judah—36
Pharaoh—37
Theotokos—38
The Widow of Niam—39

V.
Like a Speeding Bullet—43
Protanopia—44
Eyewitness Report—45
Bookstore—46
Archaeologist—47
Clerical Error—48
Wanted Poster—49
Marienbad—50
Dictionary—51
Continuum—52
Nightmare—53

VI.
From Manuel du Bocage—57
Self-Portrait—58
Insomnia—59
Camões—60
Primavera—61
Inês de Castro—62

VII.
The Spot—65
The Shower—66
Dream—67
Lover—68
Cage—69
Cocktail Party—70
International Dateline—71
Pursuit—72
Sonetos—73

I was horribly conscious of something fatally wrong.
– Melville

I

Bocage

1789

When you deserted your military post,
you fled from India as a refugee,
then sailed—where else?—to Macao off the coast
of China, at the edge of the South China Sea.
At twenty-three, you'd made a perfect mess
of your life, reinventing ways to fail,
and your future would be much worse (could you guess?):
poverty, illness, enemies, even jail.
But now, you have this momentary peace
four thousand miles from Lisbon and home,
where Camões once came to write his masterpiece,
some sonnets, but, most important, his epic poem,
and maybe on this beach, alone and serene,
he wrote, "Love is a fire that burns unseen."

The "2" Train

116th & Lennox

Suppose you wake to a Bossa Nova song
somewhere in Spanish Harlem near the park;
suppose you sit in your bed and sing along,
watching the dawn fuss away the dark.
Suppose you rise, undress yourself, and shower,
staring into the mirrors (unaware
how lovely you are), then spend another hour,
choosing your bright red dress and combing your hair.
Suppose you catch the train, like you always do,
to rumble underground for fifty blocks,
but suppose, today, the man across from you
is writing this poem on the top of a small white box.
Suppose he rises, holding a red red rose,
leans over, smiles, and says to you, "Suppose . . . ."

Cartographer

(d. 1863)

On every Brazilian map of the Amazon,
thirteen miles south of São Miguel,
above the Amor basin, you'll come upon
the tiny tropic town of Isabel.
But if you *really* travel to the place,
there's nothing there; there's nothing there
at all, but swamp, and sun, and maybe just a trace
of wind that whispers her name in the sultry air.
Because these maps descend from those once drawn
by Tôrres, the master, who clearly understood,
when he awoke alone in his tent at dawn,
that Isabel had run away for good,
so he would mark his cartographic lie,
and mark her name, forever, and call goodbye.

Chocolate

So why did Montezuma give his guest,
Hernán Cortés, that rather bitter "tea"
his Aztec farmers had carefully pressed
from the tropical seeds of the cacao tree?
And why did the Dominican friars bring
it back to Spain, from where, by chance,
the young María, engaged to the Bourbon King,
would introduce the "sweetened" drink to France?
And why, from London, did Mr. Fry present
to the waiting world the "chocolate bar," well worth
its weight in gold, and why did Nestlé invent
"milk" chocolate, the greatest thing on earth?
To please, of course, my love, watching her VCR,
emparadised, eating her chocolate bar.

Motes

He lies as still as possible and waits,
then opens up his eyes. They're everywhere.
Millions, billions of motes, dead as the fates,
hovering in the shafts of the morning air.
Detritus of the universe, debris,
the cosmic dust, polluted, dying, and dead,
an endless sinking suffocating sea
of sunlit dust that pins him to his bed.
He struggles not to breathe, to somehow withstand
their deadly assault into his lungs. He tries
to pay no notice as they softly land,
one by one, on the surface of his eyes.
Then he watches one come down. It hovers and floats.
But he can't close his eyes, they're clogged with motes.

Arrhythmia

He shouldn't, but he does. He runs up hills,
thinking about her inaccessibility,
her vanishings, her panics, and her pills,
her ever-constant instability.
He stops at Dyson's summit, staring out,
over the edge, at the alien world below,
knowing there's just one thing he cares about:
Where is she now? And why did she go?
He hears his racing, pounding, skipping heart,
its whirling tachycardia, its death-
like S.V.T.s, its sudden off-the-chart
fibrillation, and his paucity of breath.
He weakens in a wild, dizzying blur,
which feels just fine, because it feels like her.

The Puzzle House

"I think you think I don't know who you are,"
she says at the window, "but I know what I know."
She sits across her tiny, white, bizarre,
and sterile room, watching the falling snow.
He stares at the half-done puzzle on the floor:
Escher's *Waterfall*, just more confusions
for someone seldom coherent anymore,
being "aphasic" with monothematic delusions.
But now the stabilizers, clozapine,
and stimulants ignite some hope. She tries
to peer beyond the smothering routine:
"It's like a puzzle!" She looks into his eyes,
but fails. She doesn't have a clue:
"Where do you fit in? Which piece are you?"

Zermatt

In dreams, you dream of searching everywhere
for her, up every mountain track and trail
into the snow, the sun, and the rarefied air
of Aspen, the Alps, Las Leñas, and Vail.
You search each path, ravine, and winding stream;
always, she seems so close, yet so uncertain . . .
You wake. It's just another stupid dream.
You rise up from your bed, draw back the curtain,
and stare at the Matterhorn, which stares right back.
But then you notice someone standing there,
off in the distance, with a haversack,
a pink windbreaker, and long blonde hair.
Is it her? She waves, turns, and walks away.
Are you getting closer? Is today the day?

The Naughty Sonnet

Even the elegant sonnet can misbehave,
drinking champagne, like Miss Victoria,
the debutant, who "lit-up" for the Save-
the-Something Ball at the Astoria.
But soon, she loses her rhythm. Without a clue,
she sways across the dance-floor out-of-time,
humming off-key a vulgar word or two,
even singing a hideous off-rhyme rhyme,
flirting with the help, mumbling stuff,
silly, out of control, with nothing to say.
Finally, Mother arrives, "Enough's enough!"
So Vicky sleeps it off, then faces the day.
By noon, she's back-on-track, dressed to kill,
and ready to knock-'em-dead in Hamptonsville.

II

From Cecília Meireles

(1901-1964)

Cecília Meireles

The Rain Rains

The rain falls gently like a silent sleep
that calms and tranquilizes. The rain
rains with abandon. The rains sweep
down with the musical poetry of Verlaine,
which conjures a dream of a gloomy Halloween
and a certain timeless, abandoned palace
which evokes, in the vespers, the lyric and unseen
things of autumn, which poison the soul with malice.
And in that distant ancient palace, in that strange
and far-off land, in that misty mountain range,
the organs play moribund arias that murmur along
the huge and ghastly corridors with the wind whipping
beneath the cracks of the doors and flipping
the pages of missals, tomes, and books of song.

Cecília Meireles

Herod

Mannaeus, panting, returns from the cell of the dead.
He carries in his hands, as he makes his way,
the Baptist's pale and severed head,
which drips with blood on a large and glittering tray,
which he extends to Salome, and then
to Herod, Vitellius, Aulus, and everyone,
who pass it all around. But later, when
Phanuel sits alone, when the feast is done,
he stares through the torch's light and the smoky air
with a terrible silent pain, for he
can clearly see in John's prophetic eyes:
the meek pass by, one by one, out there
in the wasted landscape of the Mortuus Sea,
where the placid trickling Jordan lies.

Cecília Meireles

Spider Hole

Up where even the dust can't reach that high,
she weaves her fragile web, to and fro,
then quickly back and forth, then by and by,
without fatigue, mistake, or vertigo.
And when she's done her work, her very best,
she then shows off her magnificent web; then free
at last, the little spider takes her rest,
surrounded by her silken majesty.
The fires of the voluptuous sun ignite
her web, as she sits at its center, a gemstone,
like a glittering tawny topaz. And I believe
this spider is a philosopher, a bright
deserter from the world, all alone,
entangled in the subtle dreams she weaves.

Cecília Meireles

Joan of Arc

Firm in the saddle of her panting little horse,
she races in the vanguard of her troops as they dart
at the enemy trenches, galloping on course,
serene, ecstatic, and with a happy heart.
Her seemingly virile fingers occupy
a ringed and iron gauntlet as only she
holds high the palpitating flag in the sky
with its golden splendor of the fleur-de-lis.
Confident with dreams, and youth, and sincere
belief, the Maid of Orleans, in a mystical daze
proceeds undaunted with her missionary aims.
She smiles, and not a single tremor of fear
invades her soul, but her bold and visionary gaze
already reflects the bonfire's sinister flames.

Cecília Meireles

Coimbra Night

Enchanted night! Everything is white,
as though bathed in the pallor of opal. With lulling ease
the Mondego River seems to fall asleep tonight
and dream beneath the caressing sighs of the breeze.
Tonight, warm with love, everything's at rest,
and yet, the silvery moon wishes it knew
why it's uneasy, why it's distressed,
why it's languid and cold in the faded blue.
In the garden of the sleeping palace, where
the serenading nightingales sing
their love to the flowers, the moon paints everything
    white,
while, near the fountain, in the sighs of someone there
who's conjured the dead: Pedro, the son of the king,
kisses Inês de Castro in the Coimbra night.

III

Seaside Heights

The Boardwalk

What if you didn't see her that summer's night,
strolling along, barefoot, devil-may-care,
barely fifteen, charming in the seaside light,
with cotton-candy, with flowers in her hair?
What if you didn't follow her down the pier,
or notice that her eyes were cyanic blue,
making an ass of yourself making it clear
how *blue* they were, which she already knew?
What if you didn't make her laugh and say
what she said, winning every argument,
driving you nuts, in every kind of way,
for nineteen years (until the accident)?
What if she never became your wife?
What if you'd led a perfectly boring life?

Blood Splatter

Someone has to do it. He looks around,
checks the splattered wall, takes out his tape
and measures things, without a thought or sound,
checking every angle-pattern-shape.
It was, he could tell, a random shot in the night.
"Maybe someone hunting," he told the police.
The "vic" was pretty, female, twelve, and white,
and also his sister's only child, his niece,
who was a quiet girl, who loved her bike,
her dog, her church, skating, Christmas, and snow,
but being rather squeamish, didn't like
any book, or film, or television show
that dealt with death or violence or guns,
most especially, the forensic ones.

Post Card

"Hello!" This one's from Montego Bay:
"Glad you're not here!" She never signs her name
but sends a different card each Valentine's Day,
for fifteen years. The message is always the same,
and all the cards are beautiful: Marseille;
Nazaré; Hilton Head, Carolina;
Maui; Acapulco; St-Tropez;
Casçais; and even the wall of China.
But what did he do? She'd left him without a word,
but, every year, she sends her forget-me-not,
and though he knows it's stupid, even absurd,
he craves forgiveness for he-knows-not-what,
and wishes her nothing but love, which was, he knew,
exactly what she wanted him to do.

Reception

You knew *exactly* who it was: that unknown
guest, impeccably dressed, and slick as ice.
It stood, beneath the Böcklin, all alone,
staring in your direction, not once, but twice.
In panic, frozen, overcome with deep
disgust, you know that you're its helpless "prey";
you know that you'd do anything to keep
this useless little life you've wasted away.
It walks across the room, stares in your eye,
then turns to face your date, kissing her cheek.
She smiles, while you say nothing, not even good-bye.
She's just some pretty face you met last week.
They talk—it's all exceedingly polite—
as they walk away together into the night.

Intruder

For hours, you watch her sleep. Sitting close by,
in the shaft of light, in the scent of her perfume.
Breaking-in was easy, with the moonlit sky,
her husband away, and the kids asleep in their room.
Twelve years ago, your love went south, went bust,
she called it off. But she's got nothing to fear,
there's no venom in your heart, no lust,
no bitterness. No, *that*'s not why you're here.
Remember the time she shut her lovely eyes,
asleep in your arms, after that bottle of wine?
She stirs, shifts in her bed, and sighs,
but you're unconcerned, you're feeling fine.
You rise, you block the light, her bed goes black,
you whisper something, leave, and never come back.

Martinique

Fort-de-France

He sits on the beach watching the Caribbean sun
sink in the bay, sink in the indigo.
What do we *really* know about the one
we love? Her dreams? What did he *really* know
about her, who died that night in a terrible crash
at sweet sixteen, sixteen years ago?
In her room, with its posters of Johnny Cash,
her softball trophies, *Villette*, and *Vertigo*,
he found the travel brochures, all marked in red,
marking the beach, the bay, the high and low tide
of Martinique. So now, he comes instead,
every single year, on the day she died,
hoping she'll arise from the Caribbean Sea,
smile, and head for the beach, *plein de vie*.

Elevator

We shudder to a sudden crashing stop;
I stare at him as he looks back at me,
suspended above the thirty-story drop,
as calm in our business suits as calm can be.
We talk the market, sports, even our fears,
and once, lovingly, he mentions his wife,
never suspecting that she was my lover for years,
before she left for him, destroying my life.
A sudden bump-then-scrape jolts us hard,
then down we glide, hundreds of feet below.
In the lobby he hands me his business card,
I give him a bogus name, then watch him go,
thinking of her, her scent, her touch, her voice,
but certain now, she's made the better choice.

Fog

On the densest days, he guides his little boat
into the heart of the fog, turns off the key,
lies on the deck, and lets her float,
drifting sightless over the gentle sea,
into that all-consuming whitish-grey
of the fog, into its palpable negation,
into its wets and damps, drifting away
into its gradual world of obliteration,
where nothing-at-all exists except
the solipsism, which, in time, will bring
him to the essence of himself: swept-
away, a blank, devoid of everything,
except the thought of you, and of your death,
enshrouded in mist as moist as your final breath.

Illiterate Love Note

It lay on his desk: "Do you no how I feel?
I love you more and still yet more. Your frend."
He picked it up. How odd. Even surreal.
He read it again, trying to comprehend.
It was that pretty immigrant girl, Yvonne,
who cleaned his office every Wednesday night,
when he'd stay late and they'd talk on and on,
right through her breaks, into the morning light.
Did she know he craved to love her in every way?
That he dreamed of marrying her? That when he died,
after loving her every night and day,
he'd have, within his coffin box, inside
the inside-pocket of his funeral coat,
over his heart, this marvelous perfect note?

Impersonator

He'd been a congressman, a film producer,
a big-time novelist, a New Age quack,
a Kennedy, a Grammy introducer,
a Fox reporter, an all-pro cornerback.
Sure, it's fraud, but he's lived at the Ritz,
cruised Hawaii and the Maritimes,
done the Oscars, comped the glitz
in Vegas, and been to La Scala six times.
Dangerous? He's been arrested at least
five times and never spent a night in jail.
But it's not easy. It takes a true artiste,
absolute commitment, refusal to fail,
and far more talent than any of those fad-
ish money-grubbing celebrities ever had.

Letter of Resignation

Dear [blank]: After much deliberation,
without qualm, scruple, or further delay,
I hereby tender my formal resignation
as your lover and future fiancé.
The job provides too little satisfaction:
too many hours of unneeded duress,
a paucity of productive interaction,
uncertain working conditions, and endless stress.
Pay-wise, I'm undervalued and disenchanted:
advancement's slow, the bonus is routine,
my "on-call" overtime is taken for granted,
and benefits are few and far between.
This document, I'm hopeful, underscores
my deep regret. I'm very truly yours . . . .

IV

Sermons

(to Myself)

Eve

(Gen 3:23)

They walk to the very edge of paradise,
having already betrayed their loving Lord,
ashamed, yet willing to pay whatever the price.
They pass the Cherubim, the flaming sword,
then see the lovely world beneath their feet.
It's beautiful. But Eve knows in her heart
the sun's burning too bright in a world replete
with thorns and sweat, thistles, and dust-thou-art.
This is the battlefield, the fallen place
where Satan and his legions lie within,
in wait, with death, with every other disgrace,
within a world now inundate with sin.
Standing with Adam, in the burning sun,
she whispers, softly, "What have we done?"

Judah

(Gen 44:33)

Judah speaks before the Magistrate,
the wizard, Joseph, who decides whatever-will-be,
the Pharaoh's regent of the dynasty's fate,
who has the gift of dreams and prophecy:
"I deserve to suffer for my evil ways.
Release the boy, and I will satisfy
your judgment," he begs, then kneels, then prays,
"I'll be your willing slave until I die."
Seeing the man's contrition, his guilts, his shame,
Joseph conjures the future in Judah's face:
where Judah, in God's good time, will give his name
to the largest tribe, the kingdom, and the race,
that will pro-generate the Virgin's son,
Who'll sacrifice Himself for everyone.

Pharaoh

(Ex 10:22)

He breathes the blackness of perpetuant night,
where nothing is seen, where nothing can be done,
where darkness obliterates every trace of light:
"What kind of god can blot away the sun?"
Three days ago, when Moses cast his spell,
the locusts whirled into the seas forever,
but when the Pharaoh was firm, the blackness fell.
No matter, he'll never capitulate. *Never.*
"Father?" He hears the frightened voice. "I'm here."
Then the unseen little boy, the eldest one,
comes forth, and sensing the child's fear,
he pulls him close and tightly holds his son,
thinking, within their obsidian abyss,
"Surely, nothing could be worse than this."

Theotokos

(Luke 1:38)

Before eternity, in spaceless space,
in timelessness, in time before all-time,
the mind of God, with enigmatic grace,
conceived the Panagia, the paradigm,
the goal of generative history,
the masterpiece, of whom God said:
her seed, that incomprehensible mystery,
will crush the serpent's bloody head.
Who seemed an obscure Jewish girl until
that moment-of-moments when she would say:
"Fiat," the handmaid of her Father's will,
to consummate eternity, then pray,
humbly accepting she knows-not-what,
singing her silent Magnificat.

The Widow of Niam

(Luke 7:14)

I follow the rotting corpse, holding my breath,
prepared to bury my son forevermore;
a widow left with nothing, nothing but death,
who prays, but doesn't know what she's praying for.
Suddenly, the multitudes appear
following the Rabbi at Niam's Gate,
who meets my eyes and whispers, "Have no fear."
The funeral procession stops. I wait.
He turns to see the corpse of my lifeless son,
then calls out loud, "I say to thee, arise."
My son sits up on his bier, his death undone,
the flash of heaven gleaming in his eyes.
Then, watching Jesus leave, though shocked and numb,
I know that He's "the One who is to come."

V

Like a Speeding Bullet

She comes in like a speeding bullet, a ticker-
tape parade, a cardiac,
a Kansas twister, SWAT, 100-proof liquor,
a 4-alarm, an aphrodisiac.
She whirls into a fog, an acid trip,
a dust storm, a kaleidoscope,
a question mark, a busted microchip,
quicksand, an unmailed envelope.
She leaves you like a shipwreck, a TKO,
roadkill, a 911, a windshield bug,
a popped balloon, a spilt Merlot,
a spent shell-casing lying on the rug,
thinking, "Hey, I love her, whatever she does,
just give me more of whatever that was!"

Protanopia

The Tate Gallery

He stood in the palace of color, colorblind,
surrounded by Rossetti, Hunt, and John Millais,
yet in the visual cortex of his mind,
their pinks were blue, their reds were black and gray.
His worthless retinal cones were still immune
to color brightness—permanent, severe,
congenital—but then she entered the room
and colored his world like Morris' *Guinevere.*
He now could see the reddest crimson red,
and peacock, ruby, pink, and apricot.
"I don't know who or what you are?" he said.
"The cure," she answered with a smile. "For what?"
As drenched with color in the Pre-Raph wing,
she whispers in black-and-white: "Everything!"

Eyewitness Report

At 1:56 a.m., he saw the boat,
a "brand-new" Larson cabin-cruiser, "more-
or-less" motionless and still afloat,
maybe 120 yards from shore.
Then heard two rapid-fire shots, a splash,
and then another muffled shot "I think."
Then, rather quickly, saw "in a flash"
the Larson list and soon begin to sink;
before the naked woman rose from the lake,
"tall and blonde," vanishing into the night.
"Lovely," maybe twenty "give or take."
But he didn't stare. "It wouldn't be polite."
[Why was he there?] "Walking. I love the view—
and snooping around the lake for something to do."

Bookstore

The "celebrity" memoir was moving fast,
a *Times* bestseller. She opened a copy and checked
the index for her names, both first and last.
Neither was there. What did she expect?
That he'd remember Lisbon from years ago,
their weeks in Casçais, their lovers' pirouette?
That he'd lament the one who'd told him, "No,"
that she'd, somehow, still be his "one regret"?
She put the book back down, and left the store,
then calmly got in her car, heading uptown,
never reading in chapter twenty-four
about "Marie" in quotes, who'd "turned him down,"
who was his "only, ever, perfect love,"
whom he was "still and always" thinking of.

Archaeologist

For hours, he sat in the ancient cave alone,
stunned by what he'd found in the dust and debris:
a huge picture, frescoed into the stone,
high in the cliffs over the Tyrrhenian Sea.
It showed some red-robed figures gathered at dawn
for a sexual ritual under the shameless skies,
surrounding a naked woman, obscenely drawn,
who stared out helplessly into his eyes.
Yes, it was nearly four thousand years old,
but the face was hers, the face of his fiancée,
who was waiting in Maine, waiting alone in the cold.
Well, no one would ever see her looking this way.
He rose, chipped off her face, then sailed to Rome,
never reporting his find, then flew back home.

Clerical Error

(Personal:) "There's been an oversight.
We're sorry, and we hope we'll be forgiven.
We'd like to correct the problem and set things right
and give you what you should have once been given.
But first, we'd like to stress that our mistake
has not affected you in any way,
until, of course, it's necessary to take
away your life and let your flesh decay.
The choice is yours. We're eager to infuse
your missing soul tonight, with painless precision.
There's everything to gain, and more to lose.
So think it over and let us know your decision.
You certainly wouldn't wish to regret it.
Best wishes. Yours sincerely." "Just forget it."

Wanted Poster

He checks the poster-wall and finds his own:
"Caution." "Wanted by the F.B.I."
Just a sketch, his "whereabouts unknown,"
it lists no name, address, or reasons "why."
While mesmerized, he stares into his face,
which moves him deeply, even, almost to tears,
it seems so human, so full of warmth and grace.
He shudders. He hasn't felt this good in years.
He thinks about the artist, whoever, wherever,
she is, who seems to understand, forgive.
He wants to thank her, maybe even forever.
Why not track her down. Where does she live?
Maybe it's time for a visit? A rendezvous?
When you're on the lam, there's nothing else to do.

Marienbad

"*L'année*," she says, we saw the film together—
about that lovely woman who can't recall
the man who wishes to take her away, or whether
she's ever been to Marienbad at all.
And now, this stranger has come to take me away,
insisting, trying to make me understand:
"You promised, last year, that we would leave today."
She holds two tickets to Stuttgart in her hand.
Confused, uncertain, I can't quite comprehend
what's happening, not a single circumstance,
and yet a part of me would like to pretend
to remember, take her hand, and take a chance.
I feel, in my heart, I should be seeking out
the truth that waits within this staggering doubt.

Dictionary

Tenth Anniversary

She dreads his final gift: *The Dictionary
of My Wife.* What, she wonders, will be inside?
And so, despite the fire, the soothing sherry,
and sitting on the chalet rug beside
each other, on this seemingly serene
romantic night, she fears catastrophe.
Finally, he smiles, holding it up between
two fingertips, then places it on her knee.
Small as a postage stamp, her "monograph"
is surely the world's smallest first-edition.
She opens it up, reading her name with a laugh,
seeing his silly one-word definition:
"Perfect." Thinking, "Well, who's to say he's wrong?"
kissing his lips and loving him all night long.

Continuum

The clock goes off. Lying in the black,
somehow you sense that you've been double-crossed,
condemned, trapped within the cul-de-sac
of recurring endless time, completely lost.
The clock goes off. You startle yourself awake.
Maybe it was just some stupid dream?
Some idiotic, self-absorbed mistake?
Surely things are better than they seem?
The clock goes off. Or does it? Paranoid,
you lie in bed. Afraid, a bit in shock,
trapped within the black disjunctive void,
this hellish freak of time, you watch the clock:
your pulse begins to hyper-accelerate,
you feel the smashings of you heart. You wait.

Nightmare

When she sees me coming, no matter where,
she turns around and walks away instead;
when she hears my name, with a sigh of despair,
she turns away, ignoring what's been said.
When someone asks about "you-know-who,"
she dismisses the subject, sips her Chardonnay,
or shrugs, as if to say, "As if I knew,"
then laughs her little laugh and walks away.
Whenever the past comes up, she refuses to discuss
the "wasted years" she's trying to forget, and yet,
whenever she has her "nightmares" (her dreams of us),
she wakes with pleasure into a steaming sweat,
into the luxurious apocalypse
of love, licking the moisture from her lips.

VI

From Manuel du Bocage

(1765-1805)

Manuel du Bocage

Self-Portrait

Thin, darkly-complected, and medium-tall,
solid on my feet, with eyes of blue,
sad-faced, with a sadish appearance too,
and a nose that's uppity and not-too-small.
Unable to stay in one place, inclined to aggressions
and rage, not kindness, often lifting up
with innocent hands the darkest cup
and drinking the venom of my lethal, hellish obsessions.
The worshipper of a thousand gods. (I've lied:
a thousand girls.) Loving them even before
the loving altars where the friars pray.
Such is Bocage, in whom some talents reside,
who was struck with all these truths and more,
while he was lounging around one day.

Manuel du Bocage

Insomnia

O friendly night, in whose darkness all my laments
and sighs reverberate. O portrait of death,
the silent witness of my whimpering breath,
dear confidant of all my discontents!
Then conjure Love, who speaks only to you, and keep
her warm within your cloak, and when
she speaks, distracting you, then once again,
I'll sink into a cruel and raving sleep.
And you—vague ghosts, hoot owls, the lords
and courtiers of the dark obscurity,
and all the enemies, like me, of the light!—
help me to sleep with the dark nocturnal hordes:
I wish to join you in your dreadful conspiracy
and fill my heart with the horrors of the night.

Manuel du Bocage

Camões

(1524-1580)

Camões, how similar, great master,
I find your fate to mine. We both once found
ourselves sailing away from the Tagus, bound
for the East, to face the sea-god Adamastor.
Like you, at the murmuring Ganges, I sit in the mire
of terrible destitutions and endless terrors;
Like you, with your foolish pleasures and lusty errors,
I'm also the wistful lover of useless desire.
Scornful, like you, of all my bad luck, I grow
despondent, praying for some certainty that might create
some peace in the grave whenever my life is through.
You've been my mentor. But, sadly, even though
I've imitated you in the sensualities of fate,
I've never, in the arts, been able to emulate you.

Manuel du Bocage

Primavera

The joyful little bird, which sings each day,
revealing its soul so gently and sincere;
The river, crystal-clear, which whispers here,
while, through the rocks, it winds its way.
The sun, which strolls the diaphanous sky;
The moon, which owes its beauty to the sun;
The smiling dawn, so chaste yet full-of-fun;
The rose, which waves whenever the wind blows by;
The sweet, serene, and loving Spring,
the author of all this glory which originates
with Venus, the goddess of love, and Cythera, too.
But whatever I describe, or don't, everything,
my dear, within your presence, degenerates,
for "nothing can ever compare with you."

Manuel du Bocage

Inês de Castro

(Murdered 1/7/1355)

The sad and beautiful Inês, recalling that day,
cries out her tearful echo, which, always repeating,
begs the merciful heavens for justice, entreating
against the assassins who stole her life away.
Her cries are heard at the Fountain of Love in the hours
when the lovely water nymphs grieve and pray,
where the Mondego, recalling that infamous day,
angrily floods its banks and drowns its flowers.
The universe, itself, offers hymns above
for Pedro, the Prince, who learns of her death and races
to Inês, lying in her grave, to exhume
that miracle of beauty, kindness, and love!
He opens, beholds, kneels, groans, and embraces;
then crowns the ill-fated Inês within her tomb.

VII

The Spot

At twelve, he rises in the stale night air.
They're finally asleep. He comes down the hall,
into the living room, sits in his chair,
flips on the light, and stares at the spot on the wall.
Into its blackness, into those mysteries
where subtle paradoxes coalesce
in epiphenomenal contingencies,
like love and fear, and his utter uselessness.
Staring off through space and time to watch
the back of his watching head, reassured somewhat,
forgetting the night his wife, sipping her scotch,
said something about cleaning up that "stupid" spot,
and his reply: "If you *ever* touch a speck
of that damned spot, I'll break your bloody neck."

The Shower

"Younger than springtime," she sings, fading
in and out, for nearly a half an hour,
always the love songs, with the water cascading
over her lovely nakedness in the shower.
She's dead, of course. It's just a tape he'd made
on a lark, sixteen years ago, as she howled away
like an angel in their bathroom. And now, he played
it every morning, the best part of his day.
Sometimes he'd sing along and pathetically dream
that she was still alive, that everything was all right,
that soon she'd open the door, in the billowing steam
and towel herself off in the early morning light.
But then, the tapes fades out, clicks, yet doesn't break,
just hisses hisses like a rattlesnake.

Dream

He dreamed one night of someone else's wife,
a woman he barely knew. Waking with shame,
in a promiscuous sweat, his meager life,
he knew, in the dark, would never be the same.
But it was wrong, so he pushed it from his mind,
completely, even refusing to regret
that "guiltless" dream, that natural state inclined
to stupid seductive fantasies, and yet . . .
if he could see her again some night,
he'd fall in the pools of her eyes, observing whether
they might betray her dreams, especially that midnight
perfect dream they might have dreamed together:
a voluptuous night of abandoned clothes, champagne,
and delicious thumping love in the teeming rain.

Lover

To you, my love, in the distant future, who would
have been my perfect love: Think of our trips
together: the canyons out west (and as you stood
in wonder, I'd kiss the desert from your lips).
Or think of how we'd sail to Rio, or fly
to St. Moritz, or Prague, or anyplace
you'd like. Even ancient Egypt (where I
would kiss the sweat beads from your lovely face).
Think of our love: that steady, tender, always
kind, yet also the kind that would explode
with the secret touch of you, as within the daze
of your eyes, planets would whirl and stars implode.
Yes, we'd do all of this, and much more too,
and I wouldn't have to write this poem to you.

Cage

He hears her rattling the bars of their cage
(of their love) like a shattering deafening drum.
The whole house pulsates with her frustrated rage.
Surely the neighbors will call. The cops will come.
His head is throbbing; he needs to get away.
He steps outside, trying to decompress:
What is his perfect lover trying to say?
Does she want something *else*? Or *more*? Or *less*?
They'd built their lovers' cage with such precision
and mutuality. They were so clever,
calmly discussing every single decision,
building the bloody thing to last forever.
He enters the little chapel, sits in the cold,
and prays and prays the bars will hold.

Cocktail Party

When she appears beneath the summer skies,
across the colonnades' mosaic floor,
you stare, of course, into her whirling eyes.
"What are they like?" she asks, as if unsure.
But you hesitate. "I'm told they're 'crashing stars,'
like 'almagordos lighting up the West,'
'kaleidoscopes,' and 'depthless reservoirs,'"
she says, but shrugs, clearly unimpressed.
"So what are they *really* like?" she asks again.
"Like silly lollipops of cobalt blue,"
you hear yourself respond, and then,
you wait in the silence for a moment or two:
"Kiss me," she says, the blue intoxicating
portals now shut, the flaming-red lips now waiting.

International Dateline

Kiribati, 12/31/93

From Fiji, we gently sailed the Trades, off-shore
the Marshall coasts and reefs, to Coral Bay,
the final night of that final year before
they moved the dateline east on New Year's Day.
Arriving just in time for the "Dateline" cruise
(its "Dateline" stripe striped down its deck): a trip
into those endlessly-azured Pacific blues
to 180°, where they anchored the ship.
As we danced and drank champagne, a *Cordon Cuvée*,
rapt in lovers' love, and lover's luck,
over those shifting days that New Year's Eve
before we kissed at twelve when midnight struck,
as you stepped into tomorrow, moving away,
leaving me behind in yesterday.

Pursuit

He followed her trail from Skye to Lagos to Nice;
he heard her voice in an airport waiting room;
he nearly caught her on an island off Greece,
the cottage room still scented with her perfume.
And though he caught a bullet in Singapore,
he'll never give it up; he'll bring her home.
Her lovely sister wants her back, and he swore
he'd find her when he cashed her checks in Rome.
And now, after the close-call at Big Sur,
he's tracked her down on Capri, their rendezvous.
Of course, there isn't a "younger sister," just her,
stunning in her dress of midnight blue,
watching the surging waves striking the shore,
asking, "Well, am I what you're looking for?"

Sonetos

Tróia

Last week, stopping in the crowded mall, she said,
"Take me to Portugal, and I'll be fine."
So now they sit on the beach, staring ahead,
happily sipping their moscatel wine,
talking about the Fado song from last night,
Camões's empty tomb, and the olive trees
of Bocage's Setúbal. They feel "just right,"
enjoying each other, the beach, and the ocean breeze.
"Some sonnets?" she asks. So he reads *"Amor
é um fogo"* as the sun begins to sink,
then *"Armânia,"* then several more.
"That's more like it!" she says, taking a drink,
then smiles in the fading Lusitanian sun,
"Kiss me, first. Then read me another one."

The Author:

William Baer, a current Guggenheim fellow, is the author of fifteen books, including *The Ballad Rode into Town*; *Writing Metrical Poetry*; *Luís de Camões: Selected Sonnets*; *Fourteen on Form: Conversations with Poets*; *"Borges" and Other Sonnets*; and *The Unfortunates*, recipient of the T.S. Eliot Prize. Formerly the editor of *The Formalist: A Journal of Metrical Poetry* (1990-2004), he's the director of the Richard Wilbur Poetry Series, the poetry editor at *Crisis*, and the contributing editor at *Measure*. Previously, he was a Fulbright in Portugal, the recipient of an N.E.A. creative writing fellowship, and the winner of the Jack Nicholson Screenwriting Award. He currently serves as the Melvin M. Peterson Chair in the English Department at the University of Evansville in southwest Indiana.